ELISABET NEY

Sculptor of American Heroes

ELISABET NEY

Sculptor of American Heroes

Elisabet Ney (1833–1907), self-portrait in marble

by

Marjorie von Rosenberg

EAKIN PRESS ★ Austin, Texas

FIRST EDITION

Copyright © 1990
by Marjorie von Rosenberg

Published in the United States of America
By Eakin Press
An Imprint of Eakin Publications, Inc.
P.O. Box 90159 ★ Austin, Texas 78709-0159

ISBN 0-89015-747-2

Library of Congress Cataloging-in-Publication Data

Von Rosenberg, Marjorie, 1932–
    Elisabet Ney, sculptor of American heroes / by Marjorie von Rosenberg.
      p.   cm.
    Summary: A biography of the German-born sculptor whose portraits of such Texas heroes as Stephen F. Austin and Sam Houston are displayed in the capitol in Austin.
    ISBN 0-89015-747-2 : $10.95
    1. Ney, Elisabet, 1833–1907 — Juvenile literature. 2. Sculptors — Germany — Biography — Juvenile literature. 3. Sculptors — Texas — Biography — Juvenile literature. 4. Celebrities — Europe — Portraits — Juvenile literature. 5. Celebrities — Texas — Portraits — Juvenile literature. [1. Ney, Elisabet, 1833–1907. 2. Sculptors. 3. Texas — Biography.] I. Title.
NB588.N4V6   1990
730'.92--dc20
[B]
[92]
                                        89-48650
                                           CIP
                                           AC

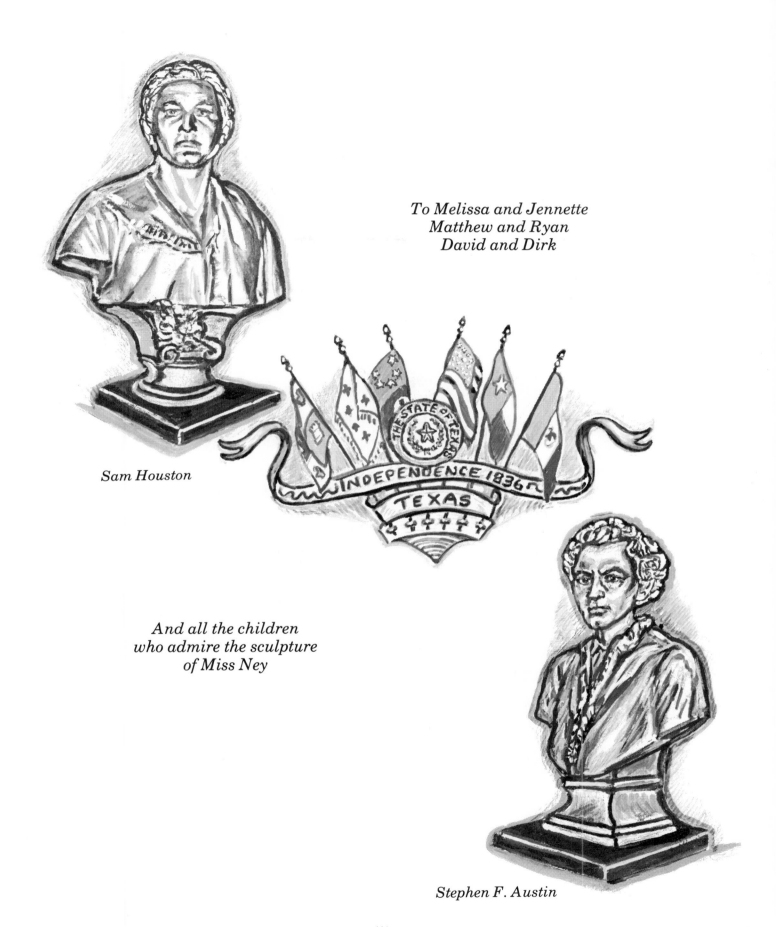

Sam Houston

To Melissa and Jennette
Matthew and Ryan
David and Dirk

And all the children
who admire the sculpture
of Miss Ney

Stephen F. Austin

A REBEL IN MUENSTER

Elisabet was modeling her little dog Tyrus in clay. She was in her father's workshop. Her father was a stonecutter. He lived in Muenster, Westphalia, Germany. He carved gravestones for the cemeteries. Elisabet was seventeen years old. She wanted to be a sculptor.

Elisabet admired her father because he worked in stone. She and her father walked to church on Sunday. They wore clothes they designed themselves. They looked different. People stared at them. Elisabet did not care what others thought of her clothes.

German girls liked to play with dolls. They were expected to be like their mothers. They learned to sew and cook and clean house. Elisabet's father and mother wanted their daughter to be a proper German girl. Elisabet was different.

Elisabet wanted to study sculpture in a big city. Her parents told her that girls were not allowed to do this. Only boys could become sculptors in Germany. Elisabet was desperate. She stopped eating. She would die if she could not be a sculptor.

Her parents went to the Bishop Mueller. They hoped he would talk some sense into their daughter. The bishop could not get Elisabet to change her mind. Her parents were forced to give in to her demands.

Elisabet went to live with her relatives in Munich. She was free to do what she wanted. Elisabet wished to become a sculptor. She wanted to meet the great people of the world.

A STUDENT IN MUNICH

Elisabet arrived in Munich. She went to the Royal Bavarian Art Academy. The director of sculpture was Herr Kaulbach. At first, he told her that she could not enter the academy. Fraulein Ney did not give up. She kept on trying. Finally, the director gave in. Elisabet became the first girl to enter the sculpture classes at the academy.

At first, the boys poked fun at Elisabet. But she gave them her hard look. Then, they respected her. She was a serious student. Her determination and talent helped her to win new friends. One of these friends was Johanna Kapp. Another was Friedrich Kaulbach.

Elisabet's fine work earned her a diploma with a gold seal from the academy. She celebrated with her friends. They went to the festival called "Oktoberfest" in Munich. They went to parties. They had a good time. But Elisabet thought only of sculpture. She longed to study under the great master Christian Rauch in Berlin. He was the most famous sculptor in Germany.

LOVE IN HEIDELBERG

It was vacation time. Johanna invited Elisabet to her home in Heidelberg. One day Elisabet noticed a handsome young man. Their eyes met. It was love at first glance. Later, they met at a party. The young man's name was Edmund Montgomery. He was a student at the University of Heidelberg.

The next few days were special. Elisabet and Edmund
met often. They explored the town. The two visited an old
castle. Edmund had rebelled against his mother's wishes for
him. He was a rebel like Elisabet. He wanted to become a
doctor and scientist. The young lovers had to part. They
swore to love each other forever.

Elisabet returned to Munich. She met the master
sculptor Herr Rauch there. He was visiting the art academy.
Elisabet was granted a scholarship to the Berlin Art
Academy. Best of all, Herr Rauch had accepted her as his
student. Elisabet was happy. She learned that Edmund was
going to study at the University of Berlin.

SUCCESS IN BERLIN AND MUENSTER

Elisabet adored her teacher. He was her ideal. His silvery white hair curled around his head. It looked like a halo. Rauch liked to work from a live model. Elisabet did too. She was one of the master's best pupils. Two of her sculptures were shown in a special exhibit at the academy.

Elisabet's parents were proud of her. They invited her to Muenster for a visit. She modeled medallion portraits of her parents. Her father liked them very much. He gave Elisabet a piece of Napoleonic lace. It was a prize possession of the Ney family. Elisabet was a relative of Marshal Michel Ney. The marshal had fought under Napoleon.

Bishop Mueller spoke to Elisabet. He asked her to create a sculpture of St. Sebastian. It was for the church museum. This was her first commission. The bishop had always admired Elisabet's work.

The young sculptor returned to Berlin. Sad news greeted her. Rauch had died. Elisabet could not bear to study under anyone else. She decided to work by herself. She opened her own studio. Jacob Grimm came to her. He and his brother Wilhelm wrote *Grimm's Fairy Tales*. Children from all over the world loved his stories. Elisabet sculpted his bust in marble.

Portraits in sculpture were Elisabet's specialty. Famous people sat for her. They were immortalized in stone. Edmund had studied books by Arthur Schopenhauer. Arthur was the best known philosopher in Europe. Edmund wanted Elisabet to create a bust of this great man. Elisabet did not hesitate. She left at once for Hamburg. She wished to meet the famous old man.

A NEW PATRON IN HAMBURG

The philosopher could not believe Elisabet was a serious sculptor. She was too pretty. Elisabet soon gained his admiration. The two became good friends. Elisabet's life would be enriched by her patron's friendship. The bust of Schopenhauer was exhibited in Berlin. Elisabet became famous. People were amazed. How could a woman achieve such greatness?

ROYALTY BECKONS IN HANOVER

The Royal King George V of Hanover summoned
Elisabet to his court. He asked her to do a large bust of
himself. This king was blind. He ran his sensitive fingers
over the clay. The finished marble bust was placed in the
Hanover Museum. Elisabet received a royal gift of apprecia-
tion. It was a diamond bracelet from Queen Marie.

Friedrich Kaulbach was court painter for King George.
The king asked him to paint Elisabet's portrait. The full-
length portrait of Elisabet was Friedrich's masterpiece. It
was hung in the Hanover Museum. Elisabet's dream had
come true. She was meeting the great people of the world!

9

SURSUM

MARRIAGE IN MADEIRA

Elisabet and Edmund decided to marry. They settled in a pretty villa named Formosa. It was located on the island of Madeira. Edmund was now a doctor of medicine. He had wealthy patients on the island. Elisabet sculptured Edmund's bust. She did a self-portrait. Elisabet loved the freedom on the island. She cut her red hair short. She learned to sleep in a hammock. She never ate meat.

Elisabet loved children. She created a sculpture of two young boys. She called the sculpture "Sursum," which means "Upwards." One boy holds the torch of learning. The other holds a key. Elisabet's theme was "Learning is the Key to Success."

Edmund would called Elisabet "Miss Ney." Elisabet would call Edmund her "best friend." The world would never know they were married.

A HERO IN CYPRUS

More famous people sat for Elisabet. She created a bust of Garibaldi. He lived on the isle of Cyprus. He would soon unite Italy. This warrior reminded Elisabet of another hero. He was named Prometheus. He was a figure from Greek legend. This hero stole fire from Heaven. Then he gave it to mankind. He was punished for giving this gift away. Elisabet began sketches for a large sculpture of Prometheus.

GIUSEPPE GARIBALDI.

PROMETHEUS BOUND IN AUSTRIA

Edmund wanted Elisabet to create a sculpture of Prometheus. They needed a large studio so that she could work on it. They journeyed to a castle in Austria. Elisabet began the sculpture of the muscular hero. He was bound to a rock. She called the sculpture "Prometheus Bound." Edmund began writing a research paper. They were both busy. They hired a housekeeper named Crescentia Simath. They called her Cencie. Cencie would always take care of their needs.

FAME IN BERLIN

His majesty King Wilhelm I of Prussia ordered Elisabet to Berlin. She was to model a portrait of Count von Bismark. The count would soon unite Germany into one nation. The bust was shown at the Art Exposition in Paris. The count recommended Miss Ney's work to the Bavarian king.

Justus von Liebig

VON LIEBIG AND WOEHLER

Some commissions awaited Elisabet in Munich. One was a bust of the famous chemist Count von Liebig. He would become one of Miss Ney's heroes. Another was the bust of the chemist Woehler. The third was a bust of the King of Bavaria. These would be placed in Munich's new technical college.

KING LUDWIG OF BAVARIA

King Ludwig II of Bavaria agreed to sit for Elisabet. He was a patron of the great composer Richard Wagner. The sculpture of this king would be the crowning point of Elisabet's career. It was also the most challenging. The king was easily bored. Elisabet put on a costume. She quoted poetry to entertain the king. This kept his attention during sittings. The king was pleased. He offered Elisabet the finest jewels. But Miss Ney was not interested.

She said, "Your Majesty, when my friends wish to give me gifts, they send me flowers." After that, the king sent her flowers every day. In time, a full-length portrait of the king was completed.

FREEDOM IN AMERICA

Things were not well in Europe. Elisabet and Edmund were tired of wars. They longed for freedom. They decided to go to America. Their housekeeper Cencie helped them pack. She would travel with them. They closed up their elegant villa. Fame and fortune were left behind. They sailed for America.

A LOG CASTLE IN GEORGIA

Elisabet and Edmund settled in Georgia. They built a log house. It was called a log castle. A son was born to them. They called him Arthur. The next year, another son was born. He was named Lorne. But the climate did not agree with Edmund. Many settlers got sick. Some died. Others went back to Germany. Elisabet and Edmund had heard of Texas. Many Germans had settled there. It had a mild climate. In 1872, Elisabet left to find a new home in Texas.

AT HOME IN HEMPSTEAD

Elisabet rode astride her horse named Asta. She gazed at her new home. It was called Liendo Plantation. The home was a historic one. Years ago Sam Houston had visited the former owner, Mr. Groce, there. Elisabet loved the old house. The live oak trees gave shade. Mockingbirds sang from the branches. Elisabet knew she would live and die there.

But her happiness did not last long. Her son Arthur became very ill. Soon he died. Elisabet was heartbroken. She gave her other son, Lorne, her devotion. But the farm needed her care, so Cencie took care of Lorne. Edmund did research in his study.

NEW WORLD SCULPTURES

The years passed. Lorne went away to school. Elisabet made a bust of him. She called it "The Young Violinist." Elisabet felt sad when Lorne left. Edmund came to her rescue. He suggested a visit with Mr. and Mrs. Julius Runge of Galveston. She began portraits of the couple during her visit. Elisabet returned home. She met a friend of Edmund's. He was Judge Oran M. Roberts. Her friendship with Judge Roberts would change her life.

19

A GREAT SCULPTOR IN AUSTIN

The judge soon became governor of Texas. He knew the
frontier days of Texas were over. He wanted his state to
become a cultural and educational one. The University of
Texas would soon open in Austin. Elisabet modeled a bust of
Governor Roberts. The plaster bust was displayed at the
opening of the new University of Texas.

TEXAS HEROES

Elisabet was excited. She had been invited to the
Governor's Mansion. The women of Texas had formed a
committee. It was headed by Mrs. William B. Tobin. They
were in charge of the Texas Pavillion at the Chicago
Columbian Exhibition. The exhibition would be held to
celebrate the 400th anniversary of the discovery of America.
Governor Roberts asked Elisabet to create statues of two
great Texas heroes. They were Sam Houston and Stephen F.
Austin. Elisabet accepted the commission. She was happy to
be working as a sculptor again.

A NEW CAPITOL

A new capitol had been built in Austin. It was made of pink granite from the town of Marble Falls. Elisabet was given a studio in the basement room of the Capitol. She wanted to become the first great sculptor of Texas.

A NEW STUDIO

Elisabet had made statues of the great men of Europe. Now she would model the great men of Texas. She needed a new studio to do this. She found a lovely site by Waller Creek in Austin. The land was shaded by cedar, mesquite, and oak trees. There was a pond. Elisabet promptly named it "Bull Frog Lake." Fraulein Ney lived in a tent while the studio was being built. She slept in a hammock.

The studio was finally completed. Elisabet named it Formosa. The word "SURSUM," which means "upwards," was carved on the cornerstone. Formosa looked like a Greek temple.

FAME IN FORMOSA

Elisabet began modeling the Houston statue first. She chose to portray him as a man of forty years. He was dressed in buckskin. This hero looked steadily out at the territory struggling to be free of Mexico. Elisabet admired the man. He stood for freedom.

She modeled Austin as a pioneer. He was dressed in a buckskin jacket. He held a map in his hands. Soon her statues of the Texas heroes would become a great success. Elisabet became known as a great sculptor in Texas. Formosa served as a gathering place for the new Patrons of the Arts in Texas.

WOODLAWN

Elisabet felt at home in Austin. Some homes were elegant. One of these was Woodlawn. It was the home of former Governor Elisha Pease. Mrs. Pease and her daughter Julia were the leaders of Austin society. Soon Elisabet became a welcome guest at Woodlawn.

NEW FRIENDS

Elisabet was grateful to her new friends in Austin. She modeled a bust of Mrs. Tobin. Mrs. Pease included Elisabet in her large circle of friends. They were all lovers of art. Bride Neill Taylor became Elisabet's publicity chairman. Elisabet made a portrait medallion of her. She gave it to her friend as a gift. Nannie Carver Huddle was an artist. She was married to the well-known portrait painter William Huddle. She would always be close to Miss Ney. Mrs. Emma Burleson was another prominent friend.

Martha Bickler was a dear German friend. She was the daughter of the landscape painter Hermann Lungkwitz. Her husband was Jacob Bickler. He was headmaster of the Bickler School in Austin. The Bickler family joined Miss Ney at her festive picnics at Formosa. The Bickler children called Miss Ney "Tante Ney," which means Aunt Ney.

TITUS AND PASHA

Miss Ney kept a pony named Titus at Formosa. The children loved Titus. They took turns riding him at Miss Ney's picnics.

Asta had died. Elisabet got another horse. He was a big Arabian stallion named Pasha. Elisabet liked to drive into town in her buggy. She also drove to Liendo. Pasha got excited on these trips. Once he ran away with her! Elisabet just let him run his course.

Then Pasha died. Elisabet was sad. She wanted to remember him. His hide was tanned. It was hung on the stairway at Formosa. Elisabet often patted the hide. A new horse would take Pasha's place.

Elisabet knew she did not want an automobile to get around in. She had once taken a ride in Monroe Shipe's car. He drove a Stanley Steamer. The car caught on fire during this ride. Elisabet cried, *"Mein Gott,* this thing's on fire!" Monroe yelled, "Miss Ney, run like heck!" And that is just what they both did.

NEW COMMISSIONS

Elisabet was the center of attention in Austin. She received four commissions for marble busts. The first was for John H. Reagan, United States senator. The second was for W. P. Hardeman, a former Confederate general. The third was for Francis R. Lubbock, governor of Texas from 1861 to 1863. The fourth was for Caroline Pease Graham.

Edmund kept busy at Liendo Plantation in Hempstead. He was elected road commissioner from his precinct in Waller County. He served as academic consultant for Prairie View College. It was the first college of higher education in Texas for blacks. Edmund also continued to work on his book. Lorne had married Daisy Tompkins. Before long, he would join Teddy Roosevelt's Rough Riders.

A TRIP TO GERMANY

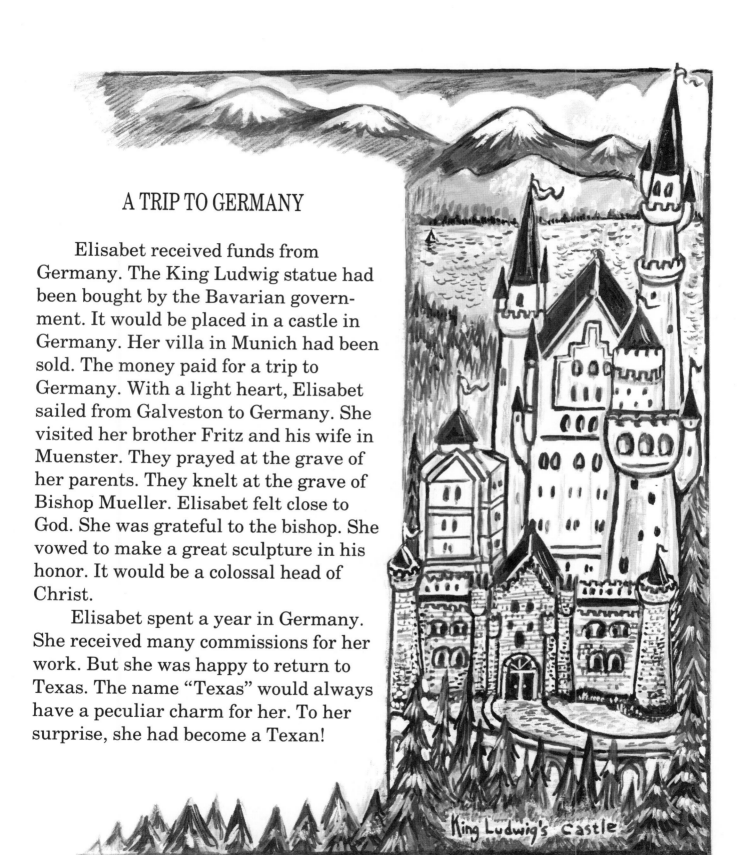

Elisabet received funds from Germany. The King Ludwig statue had been bought by the Bavarian government. It would be placed in a castle in Germany. Her villa in Munich had been sold. The money paid for a trip to Germany. With a light heart, Elisabet sailed from Galveston to Germany. She visited her brother Fritz and his wife in Muenster. They prayed at the grave of her parents. They knelt at the grave of Bishop Mueller. Elisabet felt close to God. She was grateful to the bishop. She vowed to make a great sculpture in his honor. It would be a colossal head of Christ.

Elisabet spent a year in Germany. She received many commissions for her work. But she was happy to return to Texas. The name "Texas" would always have a peculiar charm for her. To her surprise, she had become a Texan!

King Ludwig's Castle

CHAMPIONS

Elisabet needed a champion for her work. She found one.
Ella Dancy Dibrell was the wife of State Senator Joseph B.
Dibrell. Mrs. Joseph D. Sayers was another champion for
Elisabet. She was the governor's wife. They both loved art.
They fired the sculptor's ambition.

Elisabet invited William Jennings Bryan to pose for a
portrait. He was the Democratic choice for president. He was
pleased with the bust she did of him. He ordered it to be cut
in marble.

THE LEGISLATURE ACTS

Bryan was highly regarded. The legislature was impressed that he sat for Miss Ney. They appropriated money for her statues. They ordered marble statues of Sam Houston and Stephen F. Austin. They would be placed in the state Capitol. The legislature asked for another marble statue of Sam Houston. It would be placed in the Hall of Statuary in the nation's Capitol at Washington, D.C. It would join the marble statue of Stephen F. Austin there. This statue had been commissioned by the Daughters of the Republic of Texas.

A MEMORIAL FOR A TEXAS HERO

The Daughters of the Confederacy lobbied for a memorial to Albert Sidney Johnston. He was a famous Texas hero. This Confederate general had fallen at Shiloh. The legislature appropriated money for this memorial. It would be placed over his grave in the state cemetery. Miss Ney's monument would prove to be a great sculpture.

DISASTER IN LIENDO

Elisabet was happy. Her joy did not last long. Sad news came from Liendo. There was a flood. The cotton crop was ruined. Edmund was ill with malaria. Lorne had married again. His new wife was Alma Wietgen. Elisabet nursed Edmund back to health. Then she went back to Formosa. The money from the legislature saved Liendo from complete disaster.

A CASTLE IN AUSTIN

Elisabet felt her studio was too small. She added a tower.
She could look out at the Capitol. She could see the
University of Texas. A balcony was added. It was decorated
with four Texas star emblems. The finished studio looked
like a castle. Elisabet hoped it would be a museum someday.

ANOTHER TRIP TO GERMANY

Elisabet sailed for Germany again. Her plaster statues were cut in marble in Berlin. Edmund took a vacation in the Alps. Then he joined Elisabet in Germany. They felt like young lovers again. But soon they returned to Texas.

TEXAS HEROES UNVEILED

The marble statues of Houston and Austin were placed in the main entrance to the rotunda of the Capitol. Soon a grand ceremony took place. Mrs. Dibrell unveiled the statues. The public admired the statues of the Texas heroes. Miss Ney was now famous in her new country.

PORTRAITS OF FRIENDS

Elisabet was grateful to her friends. She made a portrait of Governor Sayers. She modeled a bust of Senator Dibrell. Then she made a medallion for Ella Dibrell. Elisabet hoped her busts of former governors Oran Roberts, Francis Lubbock, and Sul Ross would be placed in the Capitol.

SCULPTURES FOR THE UNIVERSITY

Helen Marr Kirby was the first dean of women at the University of Texas. The women students wished to honor her. They commissioned Elisabet to make a life-sized portrait medallion of the dean. It would be presented to the University of Texas. The university alumni asked Elisabet to make a portrait of Swante Palm. He was a good friend to the university. They also asked for a marble copy of the bust of Governor Roberts.

AN INSPIRING FRIEND

Miss Ney was inspired by a new friend. Her name was Madam Schumann-Heink. She was a famous opera singer. She performed at the University of Texas. Miss Ney presented the singer with a small plaster model of Lady Macbeth. The gift sealed their friendship.

Miss Ney was no longer young. She was seventy years old. Her greatest work lay before her. It was the statue of Lady Macbeth.

A CENTER OF CULTURE

Other artists came to Austin.
Elisabet met the great singer Enrico
Caruso. She watched Pavlova dance. She
heard Paderewski play the piano.
Formosa became a center for these
performing artists. They came to visit
Miss Ney after their concerts at the
University of Texas.

A TRIP TO ITALY

The world's finest marble was found in Seravezza, Italy. The great Michelangelo had once cut marble into statues there. Miss Ney made a trip to this place. She chose a large block of marble for the Johnston memorial. Miss Ney found pure white marble for the head of Christ. She hoped to display these pieces at the St. Louis Exposition of Arts and Science.

Elisabet had often slept in a hammock. In Italy, she slept in a bed. Fraulein Ney ate a breakfast of raw eggs. She mixed the eggs with sugar and brandy. It was her favorite meal. She needed to be strong. The stonecutters did the outside rough work on the marble. Miss Ney did the details, fine lines, and expression. Her days were filled with marble dust. Finally, the work was done. The sculptures were sent to St. Louis. Miss Ney left Europe for the last time.

A VISIT TO WASHINGTON, D.C.

Elisabet had two visits to make on her way home. First, she stopped in Washington, D.C. There, she was the guest of Congressman and Mrs. Albert S. Burleson. They took her to the Hall of Statuary. Her marble statues of Austin and Houston were on view. Elisabet met the director. He complained to her. He felt the Houston statue was too tall. He thought the Austin statue was too short. Elisabet gave him her hard look. She said, "God Almighty makes men. I only copy his handiwork. I suggest you take your complaint to God."

44

THE ST. LOUIS EXPOSITION

Her second visit was to St. Louis. She went to the Exposition. She visited the Texas Sculpture Building. The Johnston Memorial was there. She saw her bronze statuette of Garibaldi. A plaster bust of Jacob Grimm was on view. The King Ludwig statue stood before her. But the bust of Governor Sayers and the head of Christ had not been accepted. Elisabet was disappointed. She received a bronze medal for her Johnston Memorial. Her trusted black servant Horace Williams kept watch over her statues.

A RIVAL

Pompeo Coppini was a sculptor from San Antonio. He was Miss Ney's most serious rival in Texas. His statue of General Rufus Burleson was placed next to Elisabet's work in St. Louis. The general was president of Baylor University. The statue held out a top hat. It appeared to be asking for a donation. Elisabet threw a coin in the hat. She did not like having a rival in Texas.

A CELEBRATION

Elisabet was sad. The St. Louis exhibit had not lived up to her expectations. She went home to her best friend. A birthday celebration was taking place at Liendo. Edmund was seventy-two years old. His book had been published. Cencie made a raisin cake for him. They all drank a toast to Edmund. Elisabet was happy again.

Lorne had married a third time. His wife was named Sarah Campbell. Cencie took care of his children.

Soon Elisabet felt the creative urge. She returned to Formosa by train. She was expecting a visitor there.

EDMUND MONTGOMERY

SIGNOR COSIMO DOCCHI

Signor Cosimo Docchi arrived at Formosa. He was a
stonecutter from Italy. Miss Ney had engaged him to assist
her. A pure white block of Seravezza marble awaited him. He
and Miss Ney would cut the statue of Lady Macbeth into
marble. Signor Docchi enjoyed life. He drank red wine. Songs
of sunshine filled the air. He strummed on his guitar for
Elisabet's guests.

He and Max Bickler became good friends. They helped
Miss Ney on a special project. William L. Prather had died.
He was the president of the University of Texas. His family
and the Board of Regents asked Elisabet to make a death
mask of him. Elisabet could not bear to do it. She had made
one of Max's father, Jacob. It had deepened her sorrow for
her friend. So Max and Signor Docchi made the death mask
of President Prather for her. Elisabet created a plaster bust
from the mask. The final marble portrait was placed in the
Main Building of the university.

THE MAKING OF A MASTERPIECE

Miss Ney's friends had taken a great interest in the statue of Lady Macbeth. Lily Haynie had posed for the arms and shoulders. She was Nannie Huddle's sister. Alma Tips had posed for the body. Emma Reinli had sat for the portrait. A German girl had posed for the hands and feet. But Ella Dibrell was the spiritual source. She would decide on the final placement of the statue.

A SAD GOODBYE

Signor Docchi admired the statue of Lady Macbeth. He was sorry to leave when the work was done. He wanted Miss Ney to remember him. So he carved her portrait in the stone wall of Formosa. Elisabet was alone. She looked at the finished statue. The lady in white marble was so beautiful. Elisabet knew it was her masterpiece.

THE LAST COMMISSION

Elisabet's final work was a tombstone for Elisabeth Emma Schnerr of Fredericksburg. She chose a whimsical subject for the marble. The face of a winged cherub looks over the top of the stone. It views the world with wonder.

51

FINAL DAYS AT FORMOSA

By 1907, Elisabet was very tired. The work on Lady
Macbeth had taken most of her strength. Her black servant
Ben carried her upstairs. She would not come down again.
Dr. Montgomery came from Liendo. He took care of Miss
Ney. He was her best friend. Elisabet and Edmund talked of
many things before she died on June 29. They remembered
one day very well. A group of schoolchildren had presented
Miss Ney with a flag and a poem. The words were these:

"We give you this flag
  As a sign that we love you,
  For the work you have done
  For history and art.
  You will know when it waves
  Triumphant above you
  We rejoice in its waving
  With a patriot's heart."

THE BURIAL

Miss Ney was buried at Liendo. Live oak trees shaded her grave. Mockingbirds sang. Sun filtered through the leaves. She had told Edmund, "There must be no mourning when I put out to sea." So there was no funeral ceremony. A stone was placed over her grave. It was inscribed simply:

"ELISABET NEY, SCULPTOR."

Like the torch bearer in the sculpture "Sursum," Elisabet's work would light the way for future generations.

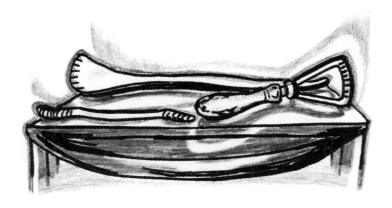

Elisabet Ney's Sculpture Process

1. The armature serves as a support for the moist clay.

2. Clay is mounded upon the armature and formed into the likeness of the model.

3. Thin metal shims are embedded in the clay.

4. To make a mold, the clay is covered with wet plaster.

5. The plaster is allowed to harden.

6. A chisel is used to pry the two halves of the mold apart at the metal shims.

7. The mold is removed from the clay.

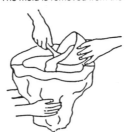

8. The two halves of the mold are joined together again with wet plaster. The mold is then filled with wet plaster.

9. The mold is chipped away from the newly-formed plaster sculpture.

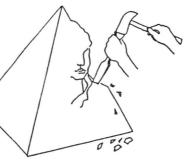

10. Using the plaster sculpture as a guide, a stonecutter copies the sculpture in marble.

11. Elisabet Ney added final details to the marble sculpture herself.

Drawings by Martha Hughes

Courtesy of the Elisabet Ney Museum

WORDS TO KNOW

achieve	colossal	immortalize	poetry
art academy	commission	jewels	portrait
art exhibit	composer	legend	research
art museum	Confederate	legislature	rival
art studio	cornerstone	mankind	royalty
artist	costume	marble bust	scholarship
bishop	diploma	masterpiece	scientist
buckskin	fame	medallion	sculptor
Capitol	freedom	model	sculpture
career	Greek temple	patron	talent
cemetery	governor	pioneer	territory
champion	hammock	plantation	torch
chemist	hero	plaster bust	university

BOOKS ABOUT ELISABET NEY

Cutrer. *The Art of the Woman.* University of Nebraska.

Fortune, Jan, and Jean Burton. *Elisabet Ney.* New York: Knopf, 1943.

Goar, Marjory. *Marble Dust.* Austin: Eakin, 1984.

Loggins, Vernon. *Two Romantics and Their Ideal Life.* New York: Odyssey, 1946.

Rutland, Mrs. J. W. *Sursum! Elisabet Ney in Austin.* Austin: Hart Graphics, 1977.

Taylor, Bride Neill. *Elisabet Ney, Sculptor.* New York: Deyon-Adair, 1938.

WHERE TO FIND MISS NEY'S SCULPTURE

A large number of her sculptures are in the Elisabet Ney Museum (formerly her Formosa studio) at 304 East 43rd Street, Austin, Texas.

Marble statues of Sam Houston and Stephen F. Austin are in the rotunda of the State Capitol in Austin. There are also statues of Houston and Austin in the nation's Capitol at Washington, D.C.

The memorial to Albert Sidney Johnston is above his grave in the State Cemetery in Austin.

Various pieces of her sculpture are at the University of Texas in Austin.

A bronze copy of "Sursum" is at the Children's Nutrition Research Center in Houston, Texas.

A marble cherub adorns a gravestone in a cemetery in Fredericksburg, Texas.

The marble statue of Lady Macbeth is in the National Museum of American Art of the Smithsonian Institution in Washington, D.C.

The statue of King Ludwig is in the Herrenchiemsee Castle in Germany.

The bust of King Ludwig is in the Hohenschwangau Castle in Germany.

Various other sculptures created by Ney are in Europe.

"Sursum" was one of Miss Ney's favorite sculptures. The two brothers are help-
ing each other as they walk upward. One holds the light. The other holds the
key. The light of their cooperation is the key to their progress. "Sursum," which
means "Upwards," brings light and hope to children everywhere.